Learning
to
Pray

The Journey Study Series

Learning
to
Pray

A Thomas Nelson Study Series
Based on *The Journey*
by
BILLY GRAHAM

THOMAS NELSON
Since 1798

NASHVILLE   DALLAS   MEXICO CITY   RIO DE JANEIRO   BEIJING

Published in Nashville, Tennessee. Thomas Nelson is a trademark of Thomas Nelson, Inc.

Thomas Nelson, Inc., titles may be purchased in bulk for educational, business, fund-raising, or sales promotional use. For information, please e-mail SpecialMarkets@ThomasNelson.com.

Unless otherwise noted, all Scripture quotations are taken from *The Holy Bible*, NEW INTERNATIONAL VERSION®. NIV®. Copyright © 1973, 1978, 1984 by International Bible Society. Used by permission of Zondervan. All rights reserved.

Learning to Pray: A Thomas Nelson Study Series Based on The Journey *by Billy Graham*

ISBN: 978-1-4185-1767-0

Printed in the United States of America

07 08 09 10 11 RRD 5 4 3 2 1

Contents

1

The
Privilege of
Prayer

T O GET THE MOST FROM THIS STUDY GUIDE, READ pages 114–121 of *The Journey*.

> *Our relationship with God involves communication—not just an occasional brief chat, but a deep sharing of ourselves and our concerns with God. In the Bible God speaks to us; in prayer we speak to God. Both are essential—and both are gifts God has given us so we can know Him. He has given us the privilege of prayer because He loves us and wants our fellowship.*
>
> BILLY GRAHAM
> *The Journey*

THINK ABOUT IT

Prayer is not a way of making use of God; prayer is a way of offering ourselves to God in order that he should be able to make use of us. It may be that one of our greatest faults in prayer is that we talk too much and listen too little. When prayer is at its highest, we wait in silence for God's voice to us.

—WILLIAM BARCLAY[1]

This is the confidence we have in approaching God: that if we ask anything according to his will, he hears us.

—1 JOHN 5:14

Talking . . . we're all good at it. We manage to communicate in the most difficult of circumstances. With the raise of an eyebrow, we can send a message that can be understood across a room. In today's culture, we're never out of touch. From e-mail to text messaging to telephones and cell phones, we communicate at all times with people from all over the world.

Yet in a culture where communication is vitally important, one form of communication seems to be on the downslide—prayer. We don't seem to know what it is and how to use it. Is prayer our drive-through window with God taking our orders? Can we use prayer to change God's mind? After we pray, does God say, "Hey, I've never thought about it that way!"? We need some help understanding what prayer is and its role in our lives.

REWIND

What are the three situations in which you are most likely to pray?

_____

_____

_____

What is the nature of your most common prayers?

_____ God, I made a mistake. Please forgive me.

_____ God, this is a big deal. Please help me.

_____ God, someone is sick. Please heal him or her.

_____ God, I can't make up my mind. Please guide me.

There was a time when prayer was one of the first things we heard in public schools, civic organization meetings, high school football games, and government meetings. Public prayer still takes place in some situations, but in many places it has been replaced with a moment of silence.

However, no one can rob you of the opportunity to pray . . . if you want to pray. But is prayer really that important? Is prayer something you look forward to or something you dread? Is prayer a token nod to God at mealtime or is it a spiritual life-support system?

Journey through God's Word

In the Old Testament, prayer was the primary means of communicating with God. In the technical sense, prayer is a dialogue between God and people. The two-way communication was significant in the call of Abraham in Genesis 12:1–3.

Through the call of Abraham, Israel was born. Throughout its history, its leaders were often seen in conversation with God. Moses had conversations with God (Exodus 3–4) and pleaded with God on behalf of the wayward nation (Exodus 32:11–13). Through prayer, Joshua was made aware of the sin in the camp but fell short when he drew a conclusion before hearing from God (Joshua 9).

David, because of his spiritual peaks and valleys, mastered the art of the prayer of confession and forgiveness (Psalm 51). Solomon prayed for wisdom (1 Kings 3:5–9). Through prayer, God worked miracles through Elijah and Elisha (1 Kings 17:19–22; 18:20–40). In Isaiah's call, we see the prophet's cleansing and commitment to God expressed (Isaiah 6).

One of the most thorough examples of prayer is the book of Psalms. Psalm 86 is a pattern of daily prayer that became important to the Israelites during their Babylonian exile.[2]

As we can see, prayer was foundational to the creation and sustenance of Israel. The prophets and leaders charged with the spiritual training of the nation were often in communication with God through prayer. This same strategy would be beneficial if applied to our homes, work, churches, and social activities.

It is never a mistake to pray, but it is a mistake to pray without understanding what prayer really is. Let's take a look at the incredible privilege we have of speaking directly with our Creator.

RETHINK

How many times a day do you communicate with each of the following?

_____ **Spouse**

_____ **Children**

_____ **Employer**

_____ Co-workers

_____ Other family members

_____ Friends

_____ People with whom you do business

_____ God

What do your answers to this question say about the importance you place on prayer?

_____

_____

_____

Prayer isn't a good-luck charm or something you must do; it is a privilege. God has allowed us this privilege because He wants to be in fellowship with us. God opened the door for communication for us; we couldn't open that door by ourselves. Jesus Christ died so that we would have direct access to the Father. There is no need for an intercessor between God and His people. At its core, prayer is simply communication with God.

Think about your most meaningful relationships. What would happen to those relationships if there was no communication taking place?

_____

_____

_____

Based on the quality of your communication with God, is your relationship with Him . . .

_____ Non-existent?

_____ Weak?

_____ Average?

_____ Dynamic?

What do you think should be the role of prayer in your relationship with God?

_____

_____

_____

REFLECT

Why do we need to pray? The reason is because the Christian life is a journey; and we need God's strength and guidance along the way. One of the major ways He supplies these is through prayer. Throughout both the Bible and the history of the church, those who made the greatest impact for God were those who prayed the most.

BILLY GRAHAM
The Journey

What does prayer do for us? We already have characterized prayer as communication with God. Therefore, prayer can be viewed as talking with God. God speaks to us in a variety of ways, but we speak to God through prayer. Prayer deepens and strengthens our relationships with God. The more we talk to God, the better we get to know Him and His expectations for our lives.

The Christian life isn't easy; therefore, we need all the help we can get. One of the most constant and valuable sources of strength is prayer.

Read 2 Peter 1:3. Substitute "prayer" for "His divine power." What does this verse say about the purpose of prayer? What should prayer produce in our lives?

_____

_____

_____

Prayer is like a power cord connecting a lamp to the electrical source. That lamp has great potential for lighting the room but, without being plugged in, is of no value. Christians who don't pray are the same. They have great potential but, without prayer, are of little value. In the Christian life, everything great that happens is connected to prayer.

Many people are glad to take God's gift of salvation but turn away from God's desire for fellowship. How would you feel if your child accepted everything good from you but ignored you on a regular basis?

_____

_____

_____

Since prayer was important to Jesus, it should be important to us. Jesus prayed on multiple occasions and tried to teach His followers to do the same.

Read the following verses and describe the situation in which the prayer took place.

Mark 1:35

_____

_____

_____

_____

Luke 22:44

_____

_____

_____

_____

Luke 23:46

_____

_____

_____

_____

Some people argue that we don't need to pray because God already knows everything we need. God does indeed know everything we need, but that doesn't eliminate our need to pray. Prayer gives us the opportunity to place our burdens at the feet of Jesus Christ.

What burdens are you carrying right now?

_____

_____

_____

_____

Read Psalm 55:22. What is the instruction in this verse?

_____

_____

_____

Read Philippians 4:6–7. What is the end result of placing your concerns at the feet of Jesus Christ?

_____

_____

_____

Because God loves us, He wants us to be in communication with Him. He desires to have a conversation with us about our day, our needs, and our desires. It's a friendly talk with Someone who knows us better then we know ourselves. His advice cannot be measured. His wisdom is more valuable than any treasure on earth. Why would anyone not take advantage of this opportunity?

God doesn't want prayer to become a fast-food drive-through window into which you speak your order, then drive around the building to pick up what you requested—only to file a complaint when your order isn't correct. Authentic prayer involves two key ingredients.

1. **Praise and thanksgiving is the first element of effective prayer.**

   In prayer, we don't give God our to-do list, then wait for Him to come through with what we requested. God isn't our servant; we are His servants!

True prayer begins with the recognition of who God really is. So, who is God to you?

_____

_____

_____

In the book of Psalms, _praise_ appears over two hundred times. When we turn our attention to God and His power, praise is the only response we can offer. We have the habit of praising pets for doing tricks and kids for doing their chores, but how often do we stop and offer real praise to God?

We respond to God based on who we think He is. What does your response to God say about your understanding of who He is?

_____ He is my errand runner.

_____ He is my fix-it man.

_____ He is my physician.

_____ He is the awesome Creator of the universe.

Read Matthew 6:9. How did Jesus view God?

_____

_____

_____

Read Ephesians 1:3. How did Paul view God?

_____

_____

_____

Praise is what God deserves. We don't give Him a high five and ask, "What's up?" We should fall on our faces in awe of Him and express our unworthiness to be in His presence. Any other response fails to recognize who He really is.

What do you first think of when you hear *thanksgiving*?

_____ A holiday with turkey

_____ Football and parades

_____ Family get-togethers

_____ An expression of appreciation to God

Let's be honest; we associate *thanksgiving* with a holiday more than with God. Yet, thanksgiving is another element of our communication with God. No matter what we don't have, we have plenty of reasons to be thankful.

Read Psalm 100:4. With what are we to come before God?

_____

_____

_____

List some of the things for which you are thankful.

_____

_____

_____

_____

Why does God deserve our thanks? Read James 1:17 and list the reasons we should thank God.

_____

_____

_____

_____

No matter what accomplishments we achieve in life, we can't take credit for any of them. Everything we are and everything we have comes from God. When we take credit for the things that happen in our lives, we rob God.

It is easy to give thanks to God when life is going well. What happens when things go bad?

_____

_____

_____

Read 1 Thessalonians 5:18. What should be your response when things don't go the way you hoped?

_____

_____

_____

Take time to stop and thank God for everything He has done for you. Get comfortable, because this might take a while!

2. **Confession is the second element of effective prayer.**

   As we already have discussed, sin separates us from God. The only thing that will restore our fellowship with God is confession. Confession simply means agreeing with God about what you have done, and then repenting of it and trusting Him for forgiveness.

When you first entered into a relationship with Jesus Christ, you confessed your sins and asked God to forgive you. But did you stop sinning? Of course not. Before you realized it, you had an ungodly thought or said something you shouldn't have. That sin requires confession, repentance, and forgiveness.

Read Acts 10:43. What happens when you ask Jesus Christ to be your Lord?

_____

_____

_____

Read 1 John 1:9. What is promised if you confess your sins?

_____

_____

_____

Make Psalm 51:10 your prayer for every day of your life. Ask God to create in you a clean heart and to renew your spirit.

REACT

Spend the next several moments in prayer talking to and listening to God. When you are done, write in the space provided what God said to you.

_____

_____

_____

Few things bring greater joy to a mother or father than hearing their baby's first words—and the same is true of God. You are a child of God if you know Christ, and He welcomes your prayers. He is much more concerned about our hearts than our eloquence.

BILLY GRAHAM
The Journey

What are three truths you learned in this study, and how will you apply each truth to your daily life?

1. _____

   _____

   _____

   _____

2. _____

   _____

   _____

   _____

3. _____

   _____

   _____

   _____

2

The Process
of
Prayer

T O GET THE MOST FROM THIS STUDY GUIDE, READ pages 121–123 of *The Journey.*

> *Ask God to give you a greater hunger for Himself and a deeper desire for His fellowship. You are a child of God if you know Christ, and He welcomes your prayers.*
> BILLY GRAHAM
> *The Journey*

THINK ABOUT IT

Prayer is the most important thing in my life. If I should neglect prayer for a single day, I should lose a great deal of fire of faith.

—MARTIN LUTHER[1]

A broken and contrite heart,
    O God, you will not despise.

—PSALM 51:17

Before we begin to pray, we first must evaluate the reasons we don't pray. Some people don't pray because they never learned the value of prayer. Maybe they lack concern for others or doubt that God will really answer.

Some people think that there is a magic formula for prayer. They believe that their prayers go unheard if they don't conform to a specific format. They fear that an improper prayer is worse than no prayer at all.

However, once we see prayer for what it really it—communication with God—it becomes much easier. God wants us to pray, and there are some elements that we should include in our prayer—not because the formula is valuable, but because we need to have an awareness of different things that affect our relationships with God.

REWIND

In the space provided, write a typical prayer you might pray.

_____

_____

_____

_____

Go back and evaluate your prayer, placing an "M" for every element of prayer that is concerned with you and a "G" for every element of prayer that is concerned with praising God. Do you have more Ms or Gs? Why?

_____

_____

_____

Most people don't pray because they think they don't know how to pray. First, praying doesn't require you to know a special language or be in a special place. God delights in the honest yearnings of our hearts. Second, God hears our prayers even when we don't know how to verbalize our needs.

JOURNEY THROUGH GOD'S WORD

In the New Testament, prayer was best modeled by Jesus Christ. Jesus prayed regularly and at critical times in His ministry. When asked to teach His disciples to pray, Jesus offered what has been called the Lord's Prayer (Matthew 6:9–13; Luke 11:2–4). Jesus offered His prayer as a contrast to the prayers of the religious leaders who were referred to as hypocrites.

Jesus offered a model of prayer in order to counteract some misconceptions about prayer. First, Jesus wanted to teach that prayer is not about being heard by other people.

In Matthew 6:5–6, Jesus warned people about the danger of praying in order to be heard by others.

Jesus also wanted to teach people that long-winded prayers could not be used to manipulate God. Jesus wanted people to trust God, not their eloquence.

Paul also was a prayer warrior. In Acts 22:17–18, we read about a time when God spoke to Paul through prayer. Paul realized that prayer is the lifeline of the Christian life (Romans 12:12) and critical to the relationship between the believer and God (Romans 8:14–15).[2]

It is apparent that prayer, when prioritized in the Christian life, is the difference between thriving Christians and struggling Christians. If you find yourself struggling, take a close look at your prayer life. In doing so, you'll rediscover the key to growing stronger in your faith.

The Scripture verse at the beginning of this lesson says that God will not turn away from a broken and contrite heart. Many times we don't pray because we aren't really broken over our sin.

We don't see our attitudes and actions the same way God does. Where God is brokenhearted over what we do, we make excuses and never consider how our sin is damaging our relationship with God.

RETHINK

What does it mean to have a "broken and contrite heart"?

_____

_____

_____

Whose heart is broken more often over your sin—yours or God's? Explain your response.

_____

_____

_____

Once we begin to see our sin the same way God sees it, prayer will become as necessary as breathing and eating. For the thriving Christian, prayer is natural and necessary. But for

Christians without a maturing faith in God, prayer is an option.

Is prayer for you an option, or is it necessary? How does this attitude toward prayer affect your relationship with God?

_____

_____

_____

If you want to change your life, you must begin with your prayer life. You must first understand that God welcomes your prayers and, second, that God answers your prayers—not always in the way you desire, but always in the way that God sees fit.

REFLECT

A dynamic prayer life requires us to understand the basics of prayer. Evaluate your prayer life based on these six guidelines.

1. **Have the right attitude.**

    Prayer is our way of declaring our dependence on God. It stands to reason that people who do not pray don't see their need for God. People who pray understand that they need God's involvement in every area of life.

Based on your prayer life, how dependent on God are you? Place an X on the line.

I don't pray.   I pray regularly.

I don't need God.   I need God badly.

Maybe you've never paired your need for God with your prayer life, but the two are intricately connected.

Read 1 Peter 5:5. If you don't pray as you should, substitute your name for the phrase "the proud." Now reread the verse. How does this verse make you feel when you substitute your name?

_____

_____

_____

Being opposed by God is simply choosing the losing side. In every situation in the Bible in which God went to battle, God won. When David faced off against Goliath and the Philistines, it wasn't a showdown between two nations; it was a showdown between two gods—the god of pride versus the God of Creation. Though David was credited with the win, it was God who really won.

2. Seek God's will in your prayers.

This is a tough one. We tend to go to God with a long shopping list of things we want or situations we want Him to fix. God will never be talked into doing things our way, if they are not in accordance with His will.

Consider your most recent prayer. What were the main things you prayed for or about?

_____

_____

_____

If God actually gave us what we wanted, we'd probably regret asking for many things we currently desire. Prayer isn't about convincing God to see things our way; it's about our being transformed so that we can see things from God's perspective.

> *God wants us to bring our every concern to Him in prayer and to be persistent in our praying. But we don't see the whole picture, and sometimes we ask for things that are unwise or even wrong. Seek God's will when you pray, and He will help you know it.*
>
> BILLY GRAHAM
> *The Journey*

Read Mark 10:38. How does Jesus respond to inappropriate prayers?

_____

_____

_____

Why don't we get many of the things we pray for? Read James 4:3 and write your answer in the space provided.

_____

_____

_____

Which of the following is correct according to Matthew 6:10?

_____ My prayer is the way I get God to do things I want done.

_____ My prayer is the way God gets me to do things the way He wants them done.

Prayer is our way of communicating with God regarding His will for our lives. God doesn't hide His will from us, but we often miss it because we do not communicate with Him.

3. **Bring everything to God in prayer.**
   God is concerned about every aspect of our lives. We need to cultivate the habit of praying at all times about everything—little and big. God is as concerned about our small decisions as He is about our big decisions.

Read Philippians 4:6. In the space below, list all of the things that you should not take to God in prayer.

_____

_____

_____

Don't wait until a crisis to pray; pray in all things! Then, when problems arise, you will be better prepared to turn to God and seek His wisdom in response to the situations you face.

4. **Learn to pray at all times and in all situations.**
   Many people grew up with the idea that prayer always requires them to be in a certain posture with their eyes closed. Maybe you are like that.

Read 1 Thessalonians 5:17. If prayer always requires a specific posture and closed eyes, how could we fulfill this verse's command?

_____

_____

_____

Praying can be done at all times; otherwise, the Scripture wouldn't tell us to do it. You can pray while driving, talking on the phone, working, listening in church, cutting grass, or watching the sunset.

5. **Trust God for the outcome.**
   In many situations, we pray and demand the outcome. We tell God that we are expecting a specific thing to

happen. When He doesn't answer our way, we pray harder and louder. We may even get angry at Him.

Why does God not always answer your prayers the way you want Him to answer them?

____ Because God is playing a game with me.

____ Because God is paying me back for something I did.

____ Because God doesn't want me to enjoy life.

____ Because God knows what I need better than I do.

God is sovereign—that means He does what He wants to do on His timetable, not ours. People have prayed faithfully for the salvation of a loved one for years before the person actually made a decision for Christ. God calls us to persevere in our prayers, not to pray once and never think about it again.

In the space below, list several people other than family members for whom you are praying right now. Beside each name, estimate the length of time you have been praying for this person in this situation.

_____

_____

_____

How long is long enough when it comes to prayer? Like we said, prayer isn't about getting God to do what we want; it's about our getting right with Him and seeing things from His perspective. God answers every prayer with one of three responses—yes, no, or wait. We can handle the yes answers—but unfortunately, we usually disagree with the no answers, and we grow impatient with the wait answers. No wonder we want to make God do what we want Him to do, and to do it right now. But God's timing isn't necessarily our timing.

6. Finally, learn to listen.

Sometimes our prayers are like the grocery list—we have things categorized and neatly arranged. Then, we make our way through the store picking up all of the things on the list.

Read Psalm 37:7. What is the danger of not listening to God?

_____

_____

_____

REACT

Do you want to grow in your faith? If you said yes, then you must make prayer a central part of your life. You must pray when you want to, pray when you don't want to, pray when you need to pray, and pray when you think you don't need to pray.

For what can you praise God?

_____

_____

_____

For what can you offer thanksgiving?

_____

_____

_____

Write out a prayer in your own words for each of the following:

Ask God to forgive you and to cleanse you from your sin.

_____

_____

_____

Pray, asking God for guidance and protection.

_____

_____

_____

Pray for other people.

_____

_____

_____

Let God know you desire to be in a right relationship with Him.

_____

_____

_____

When you have completed the tasks listed above, you have taken step one toward a dynamic relationship with the Creator of the universe. He wants to be in touch with you; will you let Him?

> *Pray most of all because God wants your fellowship and you need His fellowship on this journey He has set before you.*
>
> BILLY GRAHAM
> *The Journey*

What are three truths you learned in this study, and how will you apply each truth to your daily life?

1. _____

_____

_____

_____

2. _____

_____

_____

_____

3. _____

_____

_____

_____

3

Emotions That Defeat Us

To GET THE MOST FROM THIS STUDY GUIDE, READ pages 175–184 of *The Journey.*

A chain is only as strong as its weakest link, and so is our character. And where will Satan attack? Not where he knows we are strong and he stands no chance of victory. Instead Satan will always attack us where we are weak—a weakness in our character, an unconfessed sin, a harmful habit—so he can invade our lives and reap destruction.

BILLY GRAHAM
The Journey

THINK ABOUT IT

All emotions are pure that gather you and lift you up; that emotion is impure that seizes only one side of your being and so distorts you.

—RAINER MARIA RILKE[1]

Above all else, guard your heart,
for it is the wellspring of life.

—PROVERBS 4:23

Emotions come in all different styles. Many times, our greatest weaknesses are connected to our emotions. Satan is well aware of the places we are weak and will attack us where we are most vulnerable.

Emotions are God-given; therefore, they aren't inherently bad. It is through our emotions that we discover the difference between despair and elation. Our emotions confirm the presence of God's peace and our need to give our anxieties to Jesus Christ. We grow angry when we see injustice and delighted when we see God's power. All of these examples remind us that emotions have their place in our lives.

The problem is when emotions get out of control. Road rage and random acts of violence are uncontrolled emotional outbursts that have tragic consequences. If we let our emotions go unchecked, they will control us. But there is a way to control our emotions so that they will not interfere with our relationships with God and others.

REWIND

There is no doubt that people who encountered Jesus were emotional. How could they not be? They watched Jesus perform miracles and heard Him speak truths they had never heard before.

When Jesus called, people followed, and while some turned back, others stayed with Him for the duration of His earthly ministry. When Jesus was arrested, His enemies were emotional; they demanded He be crucified. When He was crucified, His disciples were emotional; they couldn't believe what was happening.

What is the emotion that you experience most often?

_____

_____

_____

_____

Does this emotion cause you to grow closer to God, or does it open the door for Satan to attack you? Explain your response.

_____

_____

_____

_____

JOURNEY THROUGH GOD'S WORD

One of the most misunderstood emotions in the Bible is the *wrath of God*. The term *wrath of God* represents a number of emotions. However, the general idea is God's total opposition to sin and evil. On the human level, wrath never comes across as positive, but the same is not true with God.

In the Old Testament, the *wrath of God* appears three times as often as human wrath. We must be careful not to assign to God the same version of wrath as that experienced by humanity. God's wrath never comes as the counterbalance to love. Even in His wrath, God has the ability to love beyond our understanding. God's wrath is a moral and ethical response to sin.

In biblical writings regarding the end times, the wrath of God represents future judgment (Zephaniah 1:14–15). God's wrath ultimately will be expressed in the form of swift and total judgment of everything and everyone standing in opposition to His purposes and His holiness.

In Matthew 3:7, John the Baptist announced God's coming wrath. In Revelation, God's coming wrath is pictured as catastrophic and complete (Revelation 6:12–17). Jesus said that God's wrath is directed toward unbelievers, who are condemned unless they accept God's offer of salvation (John 3:18, 36).[2]

> God's wrath is real and is something to be avoided. The first step is to accept God's offer of salvation in Christ; the second step is to live a godly life and avoid attitudes and behaviors that incite God's wrath.

Even God is emotional. Throughout Scripture we see Him express love, anger, compassion, and peace. Because we are created in the image of God, we experience the same emotions. However, because of sin, our emotions aren't perfect as are God's emotions. Whereas God's emotions can never cause Him to sin, our emotions can (and do) lead us to do things that are destructive and separate us from God.

RETHINK

What personal emotions are most effective in revealing God's character to people who do not know Him?

_____

_____

_____

Review the list of emotions you made above and circle the ones that are a part of your natural response to people and circumstances. Now explain why the emotions you did not circle are not a part of your responses.

_____

_____

_____

Our emotions allow us to praise God—but they can also ruin relationships. In many situations, our emotions lead us away from God. When our emotions are out of control, we sin. Therefore, our spiritual health is directly connected to our emotions and how we express them.

Describe a time in which you were the object of an emotional outburst. What was the end result of that situation?

_____

_____

_____

How did that experience affect you spiritually?

_____

_____

_____

In addition to being on the receiving end of emotional outbursts, we often are on the giving end. We harm people and our reputations. More importantly, we harm God's reputation when we behave in any way that is inconsistent with His character.

REFLECT

Some emotions are more dangerous than others. There are two categories of harmful emotions that are common to all of us. It is important that we get control of these areas before they get control of us.

1. **Anger and bitterness**
   No one goes through life without becoming angry. There certainly are degrees of anger that affect people in different ways. Some people grow angry and do nothing; others grow angry and do things that they later regret.

Which of the following have you experienced?

_____ Shattered friendships

_____ Divorce

_____ Abuse

_____ Damaged working relationships

_____ Problems in church

In how many of the above situations was anger a contributing factor to the problem? In how many was it a result or consequence of the problem?

_____

_____

_____

_____

_____

The Bible contains many examples of people who got angry.

Read Mark 14:71. What was the setting in which this statement took place?

_____

_____

_____

Paul dealt with people who were affected by anger. It is similar to situations today in which the fellowship of believers is damaged by an outburst of anger. The damage associated with anger is often the most difficult to repair.

Read Ephesians 4:13. What was Paul's advice to the Ephesian Christians?

_____

_____

_____

Anger isn't always expressed toward people. Some people express anger toward institutions, situations, the government, and even God.

What are some things that might make someone angry at God?

_____

_____

_____

_____

Have you ever been angry at God? Why?

_____

_____

_____

_____

Anger generally damages relationships, and anger toward God damages our relationship with Him. Anger toward God might be the result of life not turning out the way we planned. Maybe there was a tragedy or situations that we just don't understand. Growing angry toward God is our way of saying that we know better than God what we need in our lives. That's the ultimate example of personal pride.

> *Anger may arise in an instant, erupting like a volcano and raining destruction on everyone in sight. Often, however, anger simmers just below the surface, sometimes for a lifetime. Like a corrosive acid, this kind of anger eats away at our bodies and souls, yet we may not even be aware of its presence.*
>
> BILLY GRAHAM
> *The Journey*

Are there situations in which anger is justified? Read Matthew 21:12–13. What was Jesus' reason for being angry?

_____

_____

_____

_____

Jesus was angry because God's reputation was being harmed. Sometimes we attempt to justify our anger by assigning it spiritual value. We must be careful not to misuse our spirituality as a cover for self-righteousness or unjustified anger.

There is a connection between anger and bitterness. Bitterness is anger that has gone sour. Many Christians grow bitter and demonstrate attitudes that are the direct result of harbored anger.

Read Hebrews 12:15. In what ways have you been affected by anger and bitterness?

_____

_____

_____

_____

_____

What should you do if you are being harmed by your anger and bitterness? We must keep in mind that God understands our anger; He gets angry. Anger can even be converted into something positive. Both Peter and Paul were able to convert their anger into a passion for reaching people for God.

Read Ephesians 4:22–24. If we are going to change our behavior, what must first be changed?

_____

_____

_____

_____

In order to deal with anger, you must first want to get rid of your anger. Some people seem to enjoy being angry. They like causing scenes and demanding their way. At the root of their obnoxious behavior is unresolved anger.

Read Matthew 5:22. If you choose to be angry, of what are you in danger?

_____

_____

_____

_____

Some people make excuses for their anger. Which of the following excuses have you made for being angry?

_____ That person deserved it.

_____ That's just the way I am.

_____ I'm not going to take that from anyone.

_____ I deserve better than that.

_____ Other: _____

The Bible is specific about the danger and inappropriateness of anger. Take a look at the following Scriptures and list what each one says about anger and those who chose to be angry.

Proverbs 29:22

_____

_____

_____

_____

Psalm 37:8

_____

_____

_____

Choosing to be angry is like choosing to play with a poisonous snake. The risk isn't worth the potential consequences. In addition to recognizing our anger, we must be willing to seek God's forgiveness and help. Anger is a sin and, just like any other sin, it is covered by the sacrifice of Jesus Christ. Rather than just focusing on ridding ourselves of the negative attitude of anger, we must replace anger with positive qualities, such as love, patience, and joy.

Read Galatians 5:22–23. How can each of these qualities counteract anger and bitterness in our lives?

_____

_____

_____

_____

When God's Spirit moves in and takes control, anger and every other negative character trait will be chased away. After asking God to forgive us for our anger, we must take practical steps to deal with it.

What are situations in which you are prone to get angry?

_____

_____

_____

_____

Which, if any, of the situations above can be avoided?

_____

_____

_____

If you can avoid any of the situations, you should avoid them. Someone on a diet doesn't need to go to the donut store. An angry person doesn't need to walk into situations that they know will cause problems. Learn to recognize the early warning signs so that you can head off anger before it even becomes an issue.

Finally, learn to forgive others. Even when you feel as if you should be angry, choose to be gracious.

Read Luke 6:28 and Ephesians 4:32. What do these verses say about our attitudes toward other people?

_____

_____

_____

_____

2. **Worry and fear**

Fear, like salt, is beneficial in small doses. There are things we should fear. Otherwise, we might unknowingly walk into danger. Even the Bible warns us to have some fear. However, when our lives are overrun by fear, we can easily become paralyzed. We also fail to trust God when we allow worry and fear to dominate us.

Read Proverbs 22:3. Rewrite the verse in your own words.

_____

_____

_____

_____

_____

All dangers, however, aren't physical. There are certainly plenty of moral and spiritual dangers out there. We must be careful when dealing with these types of dangers.

Read 1 Peter 5:8. What does it mean to be self-controlled and alert?

_____

_____

_____

_____

Fear and worry prevent us from believing God's promises and accepting His love. When fear and worry are present, God's peace is absent. So what can we do to prevent being overwhelmed by worry and fear? First, learn to trust God and His promises. God cannot lie; therefore, anything He has promised is still true.

What are your most common reasons to worry or fear?

_____

_____

_____

_____

Read Psalm 118:6. How does this verse apply to your situations?

_____

_____

_____

_____

REACT

Fear and faith work against each other because they are mutually exclusive. If you are living in fear, you aren't living in faith, and if you are living in faith, you aren't living in fear.

What is more prevalent in your life—faith or fear?

_____

_____

_____

_____

If you are going to change the way you are affected by emotions, you must start with the following steps:

1. *Turn your anxiety and fear over to God.*
   Read Psalm 55:22 and 1 Peter 5:7.

2. *Stand on God's promises.*
   Read Hebrews 13:5, Psalm 23, and John 16:33.

3. *Pray diligently.*
   The end result of inviting God to live through you is found in Philippians 4:6–7.

As you pray, ask God to remove from you the situations that might lead you to respond incorrectly. Then remember that you are Christ's representative in the world. What you do reflects positively or negatively on who He is.

> *Emotions enrich our lives, but sometimes they also can overwhelm us or lead us astray. But we can learn to keep them in balance—with God's help.*
>
> BILLY GRAHAM
> *The Journey*

What are three truths you learned in this study, and how will you apply each truth to your daily life?

1. _____

_____

_____

_____

2. _____

_____

_____

_____

3. _____

_____

_____

_____

4

Things
That
Destroy

T O GET THE MOST FROM THIS STUDY GUIDE, READ
pages 185–194 of *The Journey*.

> *We can mask our emotions . . . we may conceal our
> true feelings . . . but we can't hide our actions. People
> judge us not by what we think or believe, but by what
> we do—and when our lives don't measure up, we lose
> their respect and they conclude our faith isn't real.*
>
> BILLY GRAHAM
> *The Journey*

THINK ABOUT IT

Integrity has no need of rules.

—ALBERT CAMUS[1]

*So whether you eat or drink or whatever you do, do it
all for the glory of God.*

—1 CORINTHIANS 10:31

Are we destined to repeat our mistakes or the mistakes of others?
Seeing the consequences of someone's bad choices doesn't seem

to keep others from doing the same things. In general, the moral decay of our culture makes people believe that there really are no consequences associated with their actions.

Today's bad choices aren't much different than the bad choices of past generations. Maybe the bad choices are more widespread; maybe they are more publicized. But ultimately there isn't anything new. People live with the consequences of their choices every day. Maybe they've been doing it so long that they don't even realize what real freedom is.

For every highly publicized example of indiscretion, there are countless others that never make the headlines. Men and women make unwise choices that prove harmful to their reputations, their families, their careers, their futures, and their witness. Maybe it's time to see these things before they happen so as to prevent the fallout associated with them.

REWIND

Describe your response when you are tempted or face a decision that might have negative consequences for you and your family.

Are you engaging in behaviors that could lead to your losing your job, family, reputation, or your home? Maybe you don't want to write down your answer, but in your heart you know how you should respond.

_____

_____

_____

The headlines tell the story of a high-profile athlete who has made a series of bad decisions for which he has yet to face any punishment. He is defiant in public and has retained a stable of high-priced attorneys to help him beat the charges he is facing. He believes he is invincible.

Maybe you are living the same way. You trust your ability to get out of any situation you face. You can tell a good story and think you can avoid being held accountable for your bad decisions. But is this true—or are you deceiving yourself?

Read 1 Corinthians 10:12. What is Paul's warning?

_____

_____

_____

JOURNEY THROUGH GOD'S WORD

What does it mean to be self-controlled? Greek words used to describe the concept are *sober, temperate, calm,* and *a dispassionate approach to life.* It communicates the idea that a person has mastered personal desires and passions.

The Bible encourages people to be self-controlled. Some of the passages that address the issue are Proverbs 25:28; 1 Corinthians 7:5; 1 Thessalonians 5:6; 1 Timothy 3:2; 2 Timothy 3:3; Galatians 5:23; 2 Timothy 1:7; Titus 1:8; and 2 Peter 1:6.

The freedom believers have does not give them license to live any way they want. Some have suggested that universal forgiveness of all sins negates the need for personal restraint. Some in Galatia apparently believed that. Therefore, Paul wrote instructing them differently.

The Bible, however, doesn't suggest that believers should withdraw from life in order to avoid temptations. This is where self-control comes in. Through self-control, those who are committed to the lordship of Jesus Christ can live with victory in spite of the temptations all around them. As a result, God is glorified and people are drawn to Him.[2]

In a world where there seems to be no restraint or control, a believer who lives in obedience to God's Word and
His principles can make a big difference. Don't let Satan
rob you of your God-given potential.

If you keep doing things that God has declared to be sin, you
will suffer the consequences. Some of the consequences will be
personal and private; others will be public and humiliating. Your
sin will separate you from God and rob you of your spiritual
vitality, and that is something you can't live without.

RETHINK

What are some of the warnings you were given as a child?

_____

_____

_____

_____

What were the potential consequences of ignoring those warnings?

_____

_____

_____

We live in a culture in which everyone is assumed to be a victim of something. Consider some of the warning labels that we see on a regular basis. We are told not to use an electrical appliance while in the shower, that the contents of a coffee cup might be hot, and not to swim when sharks are present. We are victims of fat-free dressing, sugar-free soda, and sodium-free meat. Life is a series of potential litigations.

Have you ever considered the fact that in many situations you aren't a victim of anything other than your own decisions? Most of the time we don't consider the consequences of our actions until we are in the middle of them. It's time we started thinking in advance: *What might happen if I engage in this behavior, and are the consequences worth it?*

REFLECT

The Christian faith often is misrepresented as a long list of rules that are designed to rob us of all of the enjoyment in life. It's not that way. The Christian life is not a set of rules; it's a relationship—a personal, intimate, daily walk with God.

If you live only by a set of rules, how do you make decisions?

_____

_____

_____

_____

If you live based on your relationship with God, how do you make decisions?

_____

_____

_____

_____

If you love someone, it affects your behavior toward that person. You want to please him or her and do the things that build up the relationship rather than destroy it.

Read John 14:15. What is the real test of our love for Jesus Christ?

_____ We give to the church.

_____ We are good people.

_____ We go to church when possible.

_____ We do what Jesus says.

If your obedience to God reflects your love for Him, how much do you love Him?

None   As much as possible

Though no sins are any larger than any other sin in God's eyes, there are varying degrees of consequences. Some sins have consequences that are more devastating than others.

What is Satan's goal for your life?

_____ To see to it that you have a good time

_____ To turn you away from God

_____ To whisper evil thoughts in your ear

_____ Other: _____

Satan knows your weaknesses and will tempt you. If your temptation is physical, Satan will see to it that you are bombarded with opportunities to yield to that temptation. If we are going to strengthen ourselves against Satan's efforts, we must develop four character qualities.

1. Integrity

    Integrity means that our lives match what we say. It also means that we are trustworthy and dependable.

If your private life was made visible to everyone, how would you respond?

_____ No problem

_____ Uh-oh!

If you responded "no problem," then you understand integrity. However, if you responded "uh-oh," you might have a problem with integrity.

Could people look for reasons to discredit you and find nothing?

_____

_____

_____

Read 1 Chronicles 29:17. What is it that pleases God?

_____

_____

_____

Think about the following areas of your life. In which areas do you demonstrate absolute integrity?

_____ Money

_____ Relationships

_____ Speech

_____ Possessions

_____ Thoughts

_____ Computer use

_____ Entertainment

The battle is between Satan's desire for you to be inconsistent and God's desire for you to be consistent. One of them
is winning the battle over you. Which one is it?

_____

_____

_____

2. Honesty

Honesty means we are honest and trustworthy in
all our activities. We always want to deal with honest people.

Read Leviticus 19:11. What does this verse command?

_____

_____

_____

> *Few things will discredit us quicker than a reputation for dishonesty. Once people conclude we can't be trusted, it's almost impossible to reserve their opinion. This is why Satan will do everything he can to persuade us that it doesn't really matter whether or not we tell the truth (or even that "truth" doesn't exist).*
>
> BILLY GRAHAM
> *The Journey*

People who have been dishonest in the past are hard for us to trust. Therefore, Satan wants to put you in a situation where your honesty is questioned. If he can destroy your reputation for being an honest person, he can make it difficult for people to believe anything you say about God.

Satan has a role in the world. Read John 8:44 and describe what Satan does on the earth.

_____

_____

_____

Among Christians, one of the most damaging forms of dishonesty is gossip. We sometimes share more information than we know to be true and package it as "a matter of prayer." First, God knows the situation, so we don't have to inform Him. Second, it is disrespectful to others to talk about them with the intent to do them harm or tear them down.

Read Proverbs 20:19 and 2 Corinthians 12:20. Summarize what these verses say about gossip.

_____

_____

_____

We can't be like Christ and also be dishonest; the two are mutually exclusive.

First Peter 2:22 says that Jesus had no deceit in His mouth. In other words, Jesus can't be dishonest.

What are some other forms of dishonesty that plague people?

_____

_____

_____

Some people cheat on their taxes or misrepresent their credentials. It is dishonest to steal music rather than pay for it. It is dishonest to commit business fraud. There are more ways that dishonesty affects us. The bottom line is that we must be careful that we are being people who accurately reflect God's character to the world.

3. Purity

Purity is the absence of immorality and perversion. It is safe to say that our world is saturated with immorality and perversion. There seem to be no moral restraints in many situations. The mere suggestion of moral restraints is incomprehensible to some people.

Read Jeremiah 6:15. Does this verse describe our culture? Why or why not?

_____

_____

_____

_____

God's standards have not changed. What God describes as wrong in the Bible still is wrong today—no matter what society says.

Read 1 Corinthians 6:18. What are some ways you can flee sexual immorality?

_____

_____

_____

_____

The only situation in which sex is to be celebrated is within the marriage relationship. When kept within those boundaries, sex is pure—the way God intended it to be. However, when sex takes place outside of marriage, it is the source of great heartache and problems.

4. **Freedom**

   This kind of freedom relates to freedom from sin's control, freedom from guilt, freedom from sin's consequences, and freedom from sin's power. It also means freedom from pressure from other people.

Read John 8:34–36. What is the source of our freedom?

_____

_____

_____

The freedom we have is the freedom to serve and honor God. Before we began our faith journeys with Christ, we were prohibited from serving God because we were slaves to sin. Now, however, we have the freedom to be the people He wants us to be.

Satan doesn't want to you be free; he wants you to be a slave to his purposes. He usually will tempt you with a specific sin in a specific area of weakness in your life.

What weaknesses or habits are areas where Satan might attack your spiritual commitment to Jesus Christ?

_____

_____

_____

REACT

How can you defend yourself against the things that destroy? You must focus on developing integrity, honesty, purity, and freedom. In response to this lesson, let's consider them one at a time.

Integrity means that your life matches what you say. If your life doesn't match what you say, you must change. People who are against you will recognize your integrity. No matter what, make it your goal to live consistently for Jesus Christ.

Pray, asking God to make you a person of integrity. What do you need to do in order for people to say to you the same thing they said about Jesus in Mark 12:14?

_____

_____

_____

_____

Honesty means being trustworthy. If you are misrepresenting yourself or talking badly about others, you are guilty of being dishonest.

How can you be more honest in everything you do?

_____

_____

_____

_____

Read Romans 12:17. What are some things you should not do because they are not "right in the eyes of everybody"?

_____

_____

_____

_____

Purity means being sexually pure. There is no area of life about which there is such a struggle. Men, this is an area in which you are most vulnerable. You must avoid even the appearance of any evil thought or action. Run from it. Women, you must understand the thoughts that men have when you are inappropriately dressed or act flirtatiously. Do not invite trouble!

In the space below, write your statement of personal purity.

_____

_____

_____

_____

Freedom is the opportunity to serve God the way He intended you to serve. You don't have to serve your old ways of life, your habits, or your hang-ups. You can serve God if you will focus on strengthening your relationship with Him.

Read Galatians 5:1. What will you do to keep yourself from becoming a slave to sin again?

_____

_____

_____

_____

> *Behavior does matter. People judge us not by what we think or believe, but by what we do—and when our lives don't measure up, we lose their respect and they conclude our faith isn't real. Now is the time to commit to God and seek His help to deliver you.*
>
> BILLY GRAHAM
> *The Journey*

What are three truths you learned in this study, and how will you apply each truth to your daily life?

1. _____

_____

_____

_____

_____

2. _____

_____

_____

_____

_____

_____

3. _____

_____

_____

_____

_____

_____

5

When Life Turns Against Us

T O GET THE MOST FROM THIS STUDY GUIDE, READ pages 195–204 of *The Journey*.

> *Can we honestly believe God is loving and kind when there is so much suffering and sorrow in the world? Yes, we can—but not because we have all the answers, for we don't. We know God loves us for one reason: Christ died and rose again for us. Even when we don't understand why bad things happen, the cross tells us God loves us and cares for us.*
>
> BILLY GRAHAM
> *The Journey*

THINK ABOUT IT

Life is uncertain and no amount of control or manipulation or contriving will change it.

—JOHN ELDREDGE[1]

We are hard pressed on every side, but not crushed; per-plexed, but not in despair.

—2 CORINTHIANS 4:8

Have you ever suffered an unexpected event or situation that you just couldn't explain? Maybe you asked God what you did to deserve such a fate. If you are like most people, you have asked that question more than you realize.

Bad things happen in life; it's part of living in a fallen world. But why does God allow evil? Couldn't He intervene and make life less painful for us? To say that God is in control but bad things still happen to good people is a stretch of our faith. When bad things happen, our only response should be to turn to God in faith and express our desperate need for Him. In clinging to God, we can survive even the most difficult of circumstances and, in the end, we will be able to glorify God for the things we don't really understand now.

REWIND

What is the last crisis you faced that caused you to look to God and ask, "Why?"

_____

_____

_____

How did that situation affect your faith?

_____ It made my faith stronger.

_____ It had no effect on my faith.

_____ It made my faith weaker.

Evil is real and affects everyone. Some people seem to have more than their share of evil in their lives; others seem to be immune. But no matter what it looks like from the outside, we all are affected by the evil in our world.

Think for a moment about the tragedies you have witnessed in your lifetime. From wars to terrorist attacks to the killing of innocent children, we see constant reminders that evil is all around us.

At the same time, we see evidence that God is real. We see Him intervene in situations that seem hopeless. We see people come to faith in Him when we have given up hope. God is real, and evil exists only because He allows it to exist. Maybe we can't explain why bad things happen, but we can be certain that God is in control even when it looks as if He's not.

JOURNEY THROUGH GOD'S WORD

In Isaiah 45:7, God declares, "I bring prosperity and create disaster." The term *create* might better be translated *allow*.

This isn't a statement that assigns responsibility to God for the evil that exists in the world. God is never the source of evil. However, because God is sovereign, evil exists at His discretion. If God creates evil, then the words of James 1:13 are untrue—and we know that God's Word cannot contradict itself. So, why does evil exist? Here are a few biblical reasons.

The first reason is *free will*. Adam and Eve were given the ability to choose to obey God or disobey God. Had evil not been an option, obedience would not have been a choice. Adam and Eve would have been robots.

The second reason is *punishment*. God is righteous and cannot allow the moral order to be overwhelmed by evil. Therefore, some of the evil we experience is God's judgment on sin (Deuteronomy 30; Isaiah 3:11; Romans 1:18).

The third reason for evil is *discipline*. In an effort to conform His children to His image, God exercises discipline. God uses discipline to mature His children into the people He wants them to be (Proverbs 3:11–12; Jeremiah 18:1–6; Romans 5:3–5; Hebrews 12:5–11).

The fourth scriptural reason for evil is *probation*. The faith of godly people is tested by the evil in the world. God's children await His ultimate overthrow of evil and, in doing so, reveal true faith to a doubting world (Hebrews 10:32–39; James 1:2–4).

The fifth reason for evil is *revelation*. The problems we encounter are the fertile soil in which our faith grows. Hosea's problems reveal God to a wayward nation.

The sixth reason for evil is *redemption*. Through suffering, people come to know God. The ultimate example is the suffering of Jesus Christ that produced a way to salvation for all people (1 Peter 2:21–24; 3:18).

The seventh reason for evil is *mystery*. The story of Job teaches that the one experiencing the evil and the well-meaning observers sometimes don't understand the reasons for the suffering. Job accepted his lot without understanding the reasons for it (Job 42:1–6).

The eighth reason for evil is to give us hope for God's *final victory*. True believers understand that God already has won the battle between good and evil. His victory will be fully revealed when Jesus Christ returns (2 Thessalonians 1:5–10).[2] In a world where there seems to be no restraint or control, a believer who lives in obedience to God's Word and His principles can make a big difference. Don't let Satan rob you of your God-given potential.

No matter what you are going through, you can be certain that God understands and will work through that situation to grow your faith in Him.

RETHINK

Everyone fears something that would be the worst possible thing that could happen. What is that thing in your life?

_____

_____

_____

How would you respond to that event if it really happened? What would be your prayer to God?

_____

_____

_____

When Jesus was facing the end of His earthly life, He asked God if there was any other way to erase humanity's sin (Matthew 26:39). Jesus was about to be punished for things He lacked the capacity to do. Jesus was punished for every sin of every person the world would ever know—past, present, and future. His punishment would have been severe enough if He only suffered on behalf of one person, but He suffered for us all.

Jesus didn't deserve what He got, but He willingly submitted to God's will and trusted God's control. A few days later, Jesus walked victoriously from the tomb, and the world has never been the same.

REFLECT

How prepared for adversity are you? Do you think that you will encounter problems in the future, or do you believe that you will escape life unscathed by evil? What role will God play in your handling of the problems you might face?

_____

_____

_____

_____

_____

_____

> *The time to prepare for life's disappointments and hurts is in advance, before they come crashing down upon us. Now is the time to build spiritual foundations that won't collapse under the weight of life's reverses; now is the time to decide to turn to God and follow His way when troubles come; now is the time to strengthen our faith so it won't fail in the midst of a sudden crisis.*
>
> BILLY GRAHAM
> *The Journey*

Read Ecclesiastes 12:1. What is the advice of this verse?

_____

_____

_____

What is your faith response to potential problems?

_____ If I can't handle the problems, I'll turn to God.

_____ I don't need God; I can handle things on my own.

_____ I plan to shut down and hope the problems go away.

_____ I will trust God, knowing that He can work for good even if I don't understand.

One of the most common problems we face is disappointment. It seems to come at us from all different directions.

What are three things that have disappointed you recently?

1. _____

_____

2. _____

_____

3. _____

_____

How long did it take you to come up with three disappointments? It probably didn't take very long, because disappointment is something we deal with all the time. Disappointment breeds other reactions.

Which of the following have you experienced in response to disappointment?

_____ Discouragement

_____ Anger

_____ Frustration

_____ Bitterness

_____ Resentment

_____ Depression

Read Isaiah 49:23. How is disappointment connected to our faith?

_____

_____

_____

Disappointment often is connected to external sources. When we feel as if we have let ourselves down, we often see ourselves as having failed. Failure, like disappointment, is something that we deal with on a regular basis. And, like disappointment, failure breeds other reactions.

Which of the following have you experienced in response to failure?

_____ Anxiety

_____ Stress

_____ Despair

_____ Other: _____

Whenever we feel as if we have not lived up to the expectations we have for ourselves, we experience the emotions related to failure. Disappointment and failure are closely related and can have consequences related to our faith. Once we see ourselves as having a weakness that leads to our personal failure or disappointment, it is easy to expect that to happen all the time. We must believe that we can be victorious over disappointment and failure.

What should we do when we experience disappointment and failure? Here are three suggestions that will help us keep our spiritual perspective on life's problems.

1. **Remember that God's love for you has not changed.**
   No matter what happens in life, we must keep in mind that God's love for us is consistent. Satan wants us to believe that God has abandoned us, but that is not true.

At the same time, God will not overlook our sins. When we disappoint Him, He stands ready to forgive us and to restore our relationship with Him. Like the ancient Israelites, we sometimes get in the habit of living in total disobedience to God. Like the Israelites, we can experience God's judgment and discipline.

God's love for His people isn't affected by our circumstances. Read Lamentations 3:22–23 and reflect on what this passage means to you.

2. **Learn to keep your disappointments and failures in perspective.**

   Because we can't control other people or circumstances, disappointments will come. There's nothing we can do about them.

Consider your most recent disappointment. In the grand scheme, how significant was this event?

Insignificant   Major significance

We will experience disappointment and failure as long as we are living on this earth. Some disappointments and failures are insignificant while others have dramatic effects on our lives. Whenever we experience disappointment and failure, we must be aware of any flaws in our character that might have contributed to the situation, then apply what we learn so that we can be more like Christ.

Think back to your most recent failure. What personal characteristics or actions on your part contributed to the situation?

_____

_____

_____

What do you think God would want you to do differently next time?

_____

_____

_____

3. Learn from your disappointments and failures, and—with God's help—seek to overcome them. Could you have prevented some of the disappointments and failures you have experienced? Did you have unrealistic expectations? Was there any sin that led to this event?

Read Proverbs 12:15. What is the practical warning of this verse?

_____

_____

_____

_____

Sometimes our ambition for the things of this world leads us to do things we might otherwise avoid. We get caught up in schemes and plans that are designed to take advantage of our gullibility rather than benefit us.

What is contentment?

_____

_____

_____

_____

What will make you content?

_____

_____

_____

Read Philippians 4:11. Is this verse true of you?

_____ Yes

_____ No

If not, why isn't it true of you?

_____

_____

_____

Because we are not content in life, we choose to do things we think will produce that contentment. We engage in behaviors, make purchases, and exercise options that do everything except move us closer to God. Until we learn to be content in God, we will be more and more susceptible to disappointment and failure.

REACT

When life turns against us, we must keep things in perspective. God still is in control and, if you have a personal relationship with Jesus Christ, you can experience His peace in the midst of life's storms.

Read James 3:2. How can this verse help you deal with the problems you face?

_____

_____

_____

Life will turn against you; you will have things happen that you don't understand and can't explain. When you go through these situations, you need to have a plan.

Read Psalm 25:4. Make this verse your prayer for every day of your life.

> *Sometimes God uses life's disappointments to draw us closer to Himself or teach us patience and trust. When God closes one door, He often opens another— if we seek it.*
>
> BILLY GRAHAM
> *The Journey*

What are three truths you learned in this study, and how will you apply each truth to your daily life?

1. _____

_____

_____

_____

2. _____

_____

_____

_____

3. _____

_____

_____

_____

6

When
Others
Disappoint

To GET THE MOST FROM THIS STUDY GUIDE, READ pages 205–214 of *The Journey*.

> *We need others, and without them life is not great. We weren't meant to live in isolation. God put within us a yearning for companionship—with others and supremely with Himself.*
>
> BILLY GRAHAM
> *The Journey*

THINK ABOUT IT

There is no room for the word disappointment *in the happy life of entire trust in Jesus and satisfaction with His perfect and glorious will.*

—FRANCES RIDLEY HAVERGAL[1]

Therefore, as God's chosen people, holy and dearly loved, clothe yourselves with compassion, kindness, humility, gentleness and patience.

—Colossians 3:12

One of our greatest sources of trouble is other people. We must deal with people at home, work, commuting to and from work, at church, while shopping, and in everything else we do. Our frustrations seem to rise and fall based on the amount of interaction we have with other people.

But it was never intended to be this way. God created Eve to provide companionship for Adam. Relationships are at the core of our basic needs in life. But people can be a problem. We find ourselves in a quandary—we need people, but we can't stand them! What is the right way to deal with the disappointments other people bring to our lives?

REWIND

List your three most significant personal relationships, then rank the disappointment you experience in each relationship. If you experience no disappointment, select 1. If the relationship is a constant source of disappointment, select 5.

Relationship		Disappointment			
1. _____	1	2	3	4	5
2. _____	1	2	3	4	5
3. _____	1	2	3	4	5

How do you normally respond when others disappoint you?

Why can't we just get along? There always seems to be some conflict with which we are dealing. We have friends who do things that disappoint us. We have co-workers who abandon us in our times of need. We expect people to do one thing and they do another. People just don't live the way we want them to.

That's the real problem—we want our own way! We go through life wanting things to go just the way we have them imagined. We want people to conform to our needs and expectations. But there is a problem—everyone else expects the same from their perspectives. Because we are selfish, we pull away from each other rather than invest in each other.

Journey through God's Word

We read the word in the Bible, but we really don't understand what it means. The word is *covet*, and it is an act of our will in which we have an inordinate desire to have something that belongs to someone else. In our terms, covetousness is at the heart of "keeping up with the Joneses."

In the Ten Commandments, *covet* means an inordinate desire that affects the basic rights of other people. Covetousness forces us to lower our eyes from seeing God as provider to seeing other people as competition.

In the New Testament, the prohibition against coveting was continued. Jesus said that a covetous man could not be rich toward God (Luke 12:15). Paul equated being covetous with being an idolater (Ephesians 5:5).[2] We can covet God's Word and His principles. In this case, coveting is something to be praised. However, most uses of the term in Scripture paint it in a negative light. When we want what someone else has, we limit the ways God can bless us. Covetousness and contentment are on opposite ends of the same scale.

When life is viewed as a competition, people are categorized as winners and losers. But that's not the way it is intended to be. God never wanted our relationships to be a burden; He wanted them to be a way in which our lives are enriched and made stronger. The same ways that we experience disappointment can be sources of God's encouragement and wisdom. Part of being on this earth is disappointment; we can't avoid it, so we must learn to deal with it.

RETHINK

What was the primary cause of your most recent conflict with another person?

_____

_____

_____

Read Matthew 15:19. Of the attitudes and actions Jesus mentioned, which ones are of concern to you in your life?

_____

_____

_____

Everything Jesus mentioned involves hurting someone else. As Christians, we aren't prevented from hurting people in these ways. Satan loves it when Christians engage in interpersonal conflict because he knows that the effectiveness of at least two people has been paralyzed. If he can convince us to fight with each other, we will not be effective in fighting for the cause of Christ.

Based on your current situation, is your witness for God being hindered by interpersonal conflicts? Explain why and what you plan to do about it.

_____

_____

_____

REFLECT

What does God really want us to do? Does He want us to be successful in business or have a nice car? Does He want us to invest our time at the Little League park or in a community organization? Questions like this have been at the forefront of human thought for centuries. Are we here for ourselves or for some other purpose?

Read Micah 6:8. What are the three things God said should be our priorities?

_____

_____

_____

In this passage, we see that God has some expectations of us. First, we see that God determines what is good. The concept of good is related to the character of God. In the creation story, we see God declaring His creation good. In Micah, we see God describing attitudes and actions that are good.

The second thing we see in this verse is that the believer's obedience to God's instructions isn't optional. The Bible says that God requires this of His followers. Let's think back for a moment—if you are not obedient to what God says, then you are disobedient. Disobedience is sin, and sin separates us from God. Therefore, if you do not do the following three things, you will not experience life the way God intended it to be lived.

God then offers three instructions—do justice, love mercy, and walk humbly with God. These three instructions highlight the two primary relationships of life.

What two relationships are highlighted in Micah 6:8? Relationships with . . .

_____ Ourselves

_____ Other people

_____ God

What relationship is NOT included in the instructions?

_____

_____

_____

The Bible isn't just a book of rules, telling us exactly how to react in every situation. If it did, it would be hundreds of volumes long, because every person and every situation is different. Instead, the Bible gives us a series of principles to guide our relationships. Like lighthouses along a rocky shore, they warn us of dangers and guide us toward safe waters.

BILLY GRAHAM
The Journey

Selfishness is rooted in our relationship with the person in the mirror—the relationship that is not mentioned in Micah 6:8. Notice that God told the people to focus on treating other people correctly and being in a right relationship with God.

Love God and other people is the basic principle in Micah 6:8. How could this principle affect your decisions?

_____

_____

_____

Read 1 Peter 4:8 and Ephesians 4:22–23. What is the principle found in these passages?

_____

_____

_____

If we trade in our personal perspectives on other people for God's perspective on them, we will change the way we interact with everyone we meet. When we encounter people with God's attitude, we cannot be rude, disrespectful, or mistreat them. We can't be demanding, demeaning, or critical. Our only choice is love.

Read 1 John 4:16. What is at the core of God's character?

_____

_____

_____

God's love is different from our love. The ancient Greek language uses at least four words to describe different types of love. The first is *eros,* or physical/sexual attraction. The second is *storge,* which is family affection. The third word is *phileo,* or friendship. The fourth is *agape,* which means selfless love. *Agape* is the kind of love God has for us and expects us to have for others.

What does it mean to be selfless?

_____

_____

_____

Read Philippians 2:4. How can you make this verse a reality in your life?

_____

_____

_____

We understand that it is important to love others, but what can we do if loving other people is hard to do? Scripture offers seven principles that will help govern our relationships with other people.

1. Read Mark 9:50 and list the principle it contains.

_____

_____

_____

Jesus instructed His followers to make living at peace with others a priority. That means defusing situations before they escalate into problems. The same challenge is extended in Hebrews 12:14.

Look at your own life and see if there is any fault in your life,
then confess it to God and seek forgiveness.

2. Read Matthew 7:12 and list the principle it contains.

_____

_____

_____

This has been referred to as the Golden Rule. We have seen vari-
ations of the rule and sometimes are confused as to what it
really says. Jesus said to treat others the way we want to be
treated. If you treat other people rudely, you should expect
the same. So many times we are most aggravated at the actions
of other people that are the very things we do in the same
situations.

3. Read Matthew 5:43–44 and list the principle it contains.

_____

_____

_____

We should pray for everyone—those we consider friends and those we consider enemies. If God never dismisses anyone from His concern, then we do not have the option of dismissing people either.

4. Read Psalm 141:3 and list the principle it contains.

_____

_____

_____

Once spoken, words cannot be retracted. The damage is done and the cleanup begins. That's why Scripture warns us to guard our words. This means measuring our words carefully and making sure that our words don't contradict the character of the God we claim to serve.

Read James 3:6. Describe a time when your words led to an interpersonal conflict.

_____

_____

_____

How could that situation have been avoided?

_____

_____

_____

_____

5. Read Romans 12:17, 19 and list the principle it contains.

_____

_____

_____

_____

When we are the victims of something someone did, we often seek revenge against that person. But rather than serving to defuse the situation, revenge escalates it. Eventually, the relationship is permanently damaged and God's reputation harmed. We can't allow hate to control us.

6. Read John 8:36 and list the principle it contains.

_____

_____

_____

_____

Sometimes we can't escape the past. Maybe we did something that is a source of embarrassment or leads us to consider ourselves as failures. We can't hold onto the past. If God forgives us, we should forgive ourselves and move on.

7. Read Colossians 3:13 and list the principle it contains.

_____

_____

_____

_____

We are quick to accept forgiveness but slow to grant it. However, our failure to grant forgiveness makes us slaves to the events of the past. We can't move forward while looking behind us.

Because there are other people in the world, we will experience disappointment. Because we are in the world, others will be disappointed with us. We can't avoid it; we can only seek to manage ourselves so that we respond with godliness to every situation we face.

REACT

Your life has been dramatically affected by the relationships you have experienced and are experiencing. Think back to your early days and how you were affected by caregivers, teachers, ministers, parents, neighbors, employers, siblings, and so forth.

Who are the three people who have had the most dramatic effect on your spiritual life?

_____

_____

_____

In what ways are you doing the same for other people?

_____

_____

_____

Because we are loved by God, we are required to love other people. It isn't easy—as a matter of fact, it is impossible under our own power. If we are going to love people unconditionally, we must allow God's Spirit to love through us. That means that we must empty ourselves of selfish desires and ambition.

How will you respond to God's desire to move in and take over your life? Will you hold on to the past and your old self, or will you give Him free reign? It is your choice, and the time to decide it is now!

> _We can't change the past; we can only seek God's forgiveness. Don't let the past hold you captive any longer. Ask God to help you strengthen your relationships by putting His love into action—beginning today._
>
> BILLY GRAHAM
> _The Journey_

What are three truths you learned in this study, and how will you apply each truth to your daily life?

1. _____

_____

_____

_____

2. _____

_____

_____

_____

3. _____

_____

_____

_____

NOTES

Chapter 1

1. Bob Kelly, *Worth Repeating*, 2003. Grand Rapids, MI: Kregel Publications, 274.
2. *Holman Illustrated Bible Dictionary*, 2003. Nashville, TN: B&H, 1320.

Chapter 2

1. Bob Kelly, *Worth Repeating*, 275.
2. *Holman Illustrated Bible Dictionary*, 1320–1321.

Chapter 3

1. Bob Kelly, *Worth Repeating*, 98.
2. *Holman Illustrated Bible Dictionary*, 1688–1689.

Chapter 4

1. Bob Kelly, *Worth Repeating*, 189.
2. *Holman Illustrated Bible Dictionary*, 1460.

Chapter 5

1. Bob Kelly, *Worth Repeating*, 211.
2. *Holman Illustrated Bible Dictionary*, 520–521.

Chapter 6

1. Bob Kelly, *Worth Repeating*, 211.
2. *Holman Illustrated Bible Dictionary*, 360.

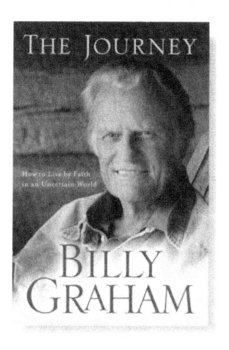

Billy Graham is respected and loved around the world.
The Journey is his magnum opus, the culmination of a
lifetime of experience and ministry. With insight that comes
only from a life spent with God, this book is filled with
wisdom, encouragement, hope, and inspiration for anyone
who wants to live a happier, more fulfilling life.

978-0-8499-1887-2 (PB)

STUDY GUIDE NOTES

STUDY GUIDE NOTES

STUDY GUIDE NOTES

_____

_____

_____

_____

_____

_____

_____

_____

_____

_____

_____

_____

_____

_____

_____

_____

_____

_____

_____

_____

_____

_____

_____

_____

CPSIA information can be obtained
at www.ICGtesting.com
Printed in the USA
LVOW13s2001250218
567844LV00021B/351/P